SO-BSJ-867

Maria Sharapova

By Jeff Savage

AMAZING ATHLETES

Lerner Publications Company • Minneapolis

Lerner Publications Company
A division of Lerner Publishing Group, Inc.
241 First Avenue North
Minneapolis, MN 55401 U.S.A.

Website address: www.lernerbooks.com

Library of Congress Cataloging-in-Publication Data

Savage, Jeff, 1961-
    Maria Sharapova / by Jeff Savage.
        p. cm. — (Amazing athletes)
    Includes bibliographical references and index.
    ISBN 978-0-8225-8836-8 (lib. bdg. : alk. paper)
    1. Sharapova, Maria, 1987– —Juvenile literature. 2. Tennis players—Russia (Federation)—Biography—Juvenile literature. 3. Women tennis players—Russia (Federation)—Biography—Juvenile literature. I. Title.
    GV994.S28S27 2008
    796.342092—dc22   2007029037

Manufactured in the United States of America
1 2 3 4 5 6 – DP – 13 12 11 10 09 08

TABLE OF CONTENTS

Grand Slam Champ   4

A Tough Start   9

Golden Girl   14

Maria Mania   18

Reaching the Top   24

Selected Career Highlights   29
Glossary   30
Further Reading & Websites   31
Index   32

Maria slams back her opponent's shot in the 2006 U.S. Open final.

GRAND SLAM CHAMP

Nineteen-year-old Maria Sharapova bent down at the **baseline**. She stared across the net as her **opponent** got ready to **serve**. The ball came toward Maria. She stood to her full six-foot-two-inches and swung her racket hard. She blasted a **return** and let out a huge scream. The ball skidded across the court for a **winner**.

Maria was playing in the 2006 U.S. Open **final**. The U.S. Open is the last of four major tennis **tournaments**—called **Grand Slams**—played each year.

When Maria played in the 2006 final, she was already famous. People saw pictures of her everywhere. The pictures were on billboards, on magazine covers, and in TV ads. Maria was one of the most popular players in tennis.

Her opponent was talented Justine Henin. Henin was playing in her fourth straight Grand Slam final. She had played Maria five times before and had won four of the matches. Before the final, someone reminded Maria that she had only beaten Henin once. She smiled and said, "I look forward to beating her again." Maria had confidence!

Henin served again. Maria smacked a **forehand** shot right back at her. Henin's **backhand** shot went into the net. Maria had **broken serve** to take a five-games-to-four (5–4) lead in the first **set**. She needed only one more game to win the set.

Then Maria got her turn to serve. *Crack!* With a powerful swat, the yellow ball sailed in a blur at nearly 115 miles per hour. Henin

Maria's opponent, Justine Henin, chases down a return.

Maria smacks a forehand back to Henin.

was barely able to return it. Maria smashed a forehand while letting out another scream. Henin couldn't reach the ball. A few points later, Maria finished the game with a monster serve. Maria won the first set, 6–4.

Maria attacked even harder in the second set. She hit shots at Henin from all angles. She chased down ball after ball. Henin couldn't keep up. Maria won the second set by the same score—6–4. She was the U.S. Open champion!

Maria hugs the championship trophy after her 2006 U.S. Open victory.

When Maria was three years old, her parents moved from Siberia to Sochi *(above)*. The town lies in southwestern Russia.

A TOUGH START

Maria was born April 19, 1987, to Yuri and Yelena Sharapova. Her family lived in Siberia, a large region within Russia. Yuri was a construction worker. Yelena stayed home to raise Maria, their only child.

Yuri became friends with the father of Yevgeny Kafelnikov, a Russian **professional** tennis player. In 1991, Kafelnikov's father gave Maria a tennis racket as a gift. She practiced hitting tennis balls against the side of her house. In 1993, when Maria was six, her father took her to a children's tennis clinic in Moscow, the Russian capital. Martina Navratilova, a great female tennis player, was there. She saw Maria

By 1993, Martina Navratilova *(below)* had won eighteen Grand Slam singles titles.

hitting balls. "She has talent," Navratilova told Maria's father.

Yuri decided to get expert coaching for Maria. In 1995, he packed up a few belongings and flew with Maria to the United States. In Bradenton, Florida, he took her to the Nick Bollettieri Tennis Academy. The school was famous for training many stars, including Andre Agassi and Monica Seles. "In the beginning it was tough to tell how good she was," Coach Bollettieri said. Eventually, though, Maria got into the academy. Yuri had to work several jobs to pay her **tuition**.

Yuri and Maria came to the United States with little money. Neither spoke English. They had to ride several buses to reach the tennis academy. Maria didn't get into the academy right away.

Maria and her father *(left)* are very close.

Maria lived in a **dormitory** with older girls. Yuri moved into an apartment one mile away. The family couldn't afford to buy a car. So Yuri walked to work and to see Maria every day. Maria's mother stayed in Russia until she could get the paperwork that let her come to America.

Maria went to school at the academy. She spoke little English. Her speech was awkward.

The other students teased her. She was especially lonely at the dormitory. "I had only myself as company," she said.

Maria worked hard at tennis. She was tall for her age. So she struggled to keep her balance and smooth movement on the court. The other girls bullied her. "It just made me tougher," she said. Maria's **agent**, Max Eisenbud, remembers how hard it was for Maria and her father. "Yuri calls it survival," Eisenbud said. "It was two very tough years. They don't forget what it was like."

Trainer Nick Bollettieri *(right)* poses with Maria before a match.

GOLDEN GIRL

Over time, Maria blossomed as a tennis player. In 1996, when she was nine years old, the academy began paying her tuition. She started competing in junior tennis events. In 1997, Maria played in the Eddie Herr

International Junior Championships for kids fourteen and under. She beat a strong player named Bernice Burlet, 6–3, 6–4. Maria was only ten years old!

A year later, she joined the International Management Group (IMG). IMG would represent her in any tennis deals. In exchange, Maria got free shoes and tennis rackets.

At the same time, Maria started traveling to Southern California for lessons from famed coach Robert Lansdorp. "I would get bored after hitting four balls in a row in one corner, and he made me hit 100," said Maria. "He taught me patience and consistency and drive."

Maria plays tennis right-handed. But she is a natural lefty. When she was ten years old, she started playing left-handed. After six months, she switched back.

Daily practice lasted six hours. The hard work paid off. Maria won tournaments often. The tennis world was learning about this spaghetti-thin girl with the powerful game and fierce desire.

Starting in March 2001, Maria grew quickly. In one year, she sprouted from five-foot-three inches to five-foot-nine! Maria became the youngest-ever girls' finalist at the Australian Open Junior Championship. She swept through the first four rounds without losing a set. She lost in the final, 6–0, 7–5. That same year, at age 14, Maria turned professional.

Soon after, she competed in her first pro tournament

Maria's legs grew so fast that she suffered from Osgood-Slatter disease. The illness made her knees hurt. She couldn't do running drills. Over time, she outgrew the disease.

Maria stretches her long legs during practice.

at Indian Wells, California. She won her first match. She met the great Monica Seles in the second round. Seles whipped her 6–0, 6–2. "For her age, she's just great!" said Seles. Maria figured she had a long way to go. She said, "Today I learned there is a big difference between a junior and a pro . . . a big difference." The Women's Tennis Association (WTA) **ranked** Maria for the first time. She was number 532.

Maria yells as she makes a forehand shot at the 2003 Australian Open.

MARIA MANIA

In her early pro career, Maria lost before she won. In 2003, she made it to the Australian Open, a Grand Slam event. She lost in the first round. In fact, in each of her next four pro tournaments, she lost in the first round. But Maria didn't sulk. She stayed positive.

Finally, midway through the year in Birmingham, England, she won her first four matches. She reached the **semifinal** round before losing. This performance pushed her to number 88 in the rankings.

At Wimbledon, the oldest Grand Slam, she reached the third round. She won a match at the U.S. Open. On October 5, 2003, at age sixteen, she won her first tournament in Tokyo, Japan. She was ranked number 33. One month later, she won her second tournament in Quebec, Canada. She was on her way!

Maria battles Yugoslavia's Jelena Dokic at Wimbledon in 2003.

Maria was loud on the court. She grunted when she hit the ball. On big swings, she screamed. Opponents sometimes complained. Maria said she couldn't help it. She got the nickname the Queen of Screams.

One person was even louder than Maria—her father. Yuri yelled from the stands and was often warned to quiet down.

Maria winds up for a backhand return to Monica Seles in a 2003 match.

Maria stayed focused on tennis. She started 2004 ranked number 31 in the world. She ended the year at number 4! She got to the third round at the Australian Open. She also reached her first-ever Grand Slam **quarterfinal** at the French Open. "I don't think anything can stop me," she said, "unless I lose."

At Wimbledon, she rolled through the first four rounds. In the semifinals, she beat former champion Lindsay Davenport. "I had control of the match," said Davenport, "and she took it from me."

With her height, blonde hair, and green eyes, Maria looks like a fashion model. Companies have asked her to model for them. She also started to have her tennis outfits specially designed for her.

Serena Williams *(bottom)* watches Maria as she serves at Wimbledon in 2004.

Maria played two-time defending champion Serena Williams in the final. Maria won the first set, 6–1. She trailed 2–4 in the second set. She focused harder. She won four straight games to win the title. Maria could hardly believe it. "I'm on my knees celebrating," she said, "and I'm thinking, 'What have I just done?'" She was the third-youngest champion ever at Wimbledon.

Maria became an instant megastar. Photographers followed her everywhere. She appeared on TV talk shows. Dozens of companies begged her to help sell their products. IMG created Team Sharapova. This group handles her deals and publicity. Maria signed sponsorships with makers of cell phones, cameras, cars, watches, soft drinks, toothpaste, and, of course, tennis rackets. She even had a perfume named after her.

Soon she was earning $22 million a year. She was among the highest-paid female athletes in the world. "I do feel like I'm being pulled in many different directions," said Maria. "It's been amazing. It was hard at first, but I've been enjoying every second of it."

Straining against a resistance band, Maria stretches her arms during practice at Wimbledon in 2005.

REACHING THE TOP

Maria still gave her full attention to tennis. "My next goal is to be number one in the world," she said. She increased her workouts to eight hours a day. She ate healthy foods. In 2005, she won three singles titles. She got to the semifinals in three of the four Grand

Slams. In August, she reached her goal. She was ranked number 1. She was the first female player from Russia to be the top player in the world. "It's a dream come true," she said. "I was trying to tell myself not to worry about it, that it's not important. But you know, once you get there, it's, like, wow!"

In 2006, shoulder and ankle injuries slowed Maria. But she still won five tournaments. Her biggest, of course, was the U.S. Open. "There's nothing like winning your first major," she said. "But to win your second, it's kind of like a cherry on the cake. But there are a lot more cherries that I'm gonna put on that cake."

Maria won two 2006 ESPY sports awards. She was named Best International Female Athlete and Best Female Tennis Player.

Maria's website names three men with whom she'd like to play mixed doubles. In order, they are former tennis star John McEnroe, movie-spy James Bond, and Vladimir Putin (president of Russia).

In 2007, she tried hard to win those extra cherries. She made it to the final at the Australian Open. But she lost to Serena Williams. She got to the semifinal at the French Open. She didn't do as well at Wimbledon and the U.S. Open. But Maria never gives up. She's ready to tackle more tournaments in 2008 and beyond.

Maria lives with her parents in a big house in Florida. She drives fancy cars and wears cool outfits. But she also shares much of her wealth. She has donated millions of dollars to good causes in Russia and the United States. She formed a foundation to help poor, at-risk children. "One of the greatest things about being an athlete and making money," Maria says, "is realizing that you can help the world, especially children, who I absolutely love working with."

Maria joins children in Melbourne, Australia, to encourage them to take part in sports.

Maria is sure she'll never act spoiled. "The way that my parents raised me and the way my life has gone, I've come to appreciate things. . . . When I was younger I didn't get things the easy way," she says. "Whatever my family and I have now, we've all worked for it. We know how hard it is to get it and we know how easy it is to lose it."

Selected Career Highlights

2007
Reached the singles final of the Australian Open
Reached the semifinals of the French Open
Ended the year ranked number 4

2006
Won the singles title at the U.S. Open
Reached the semifinals at the Australian Open
  and Wimbledon
Won ESPY for Best Female Tennis Player
Won ESPY for Best International Female Athlete
Ended the year ranked number 2

2005
Reached the semifinals at the Australian Open,
  Wimbledon, and the U.S. Open
Reached the quarterfinals at the French Open
Ranked number 1 for the first time
Won ESPY for Best Female Tennis Player
Ended the year ranked number 4

2004
Won the singles title at Wimbledon
Reached the quarterfinals at the French Open
Named Tour Player of the Year
Named Most Improved Player of the Year
Ended the year ranked number 4

2003
Reached fourth round at Wimbledon
Won first WTA tournament in Tokyo, Japan
Ended the year ranked number 32

2002
Won first professional tournament in Japan
Ended the year ranked number 186

2001
Turned professional
Played first professional tournament

2000
Won Eddie Herr International Junior Championships (for girls
  sixteen and under)

Glossary

agent: a person or group that an athlete hires to handle the athlete's contracts and publicity

backhand: hitting the ball while holding the racket so that the back of the hand is facing the target

baseline: the line that marks the back end of a tennis court

broken serve: when the player receiving the serves wins the game

dormitory: a large building with bedrooms that house many students

final: the round in a singles tournament in which only two players remain

forehand: hitting the ball while holding the racket so that the palm of the hand is facing the target

Grand Slams: four tennis championships played around the world each year. The events are the Australian Open, the French Open, Wimbledon (in Great Britain), and the U.S. Open.

opponent: the other player in a match

professional: being able to play in tournaments for money

quarterfinal: the round in a singles tournament in which eight players remain

rank: to give a number to a professional player based on performance in tournaments. The lower the number is, the better the ranking.

return: a shot made in answer to the opponent's serve

semifinal: the round in a singles tournament in which four players remain

serve: the hit of a tennis ball that starts each point in a tennis game

set: in a tennis match, a group of six or more games. Women's tennis matches have a maximum of three sets.

singles: a tennis match that pits one player against another

tournaments: a competition in which a series of games determines the winning player

tuition: money paid to a school so a student can be taught there

winner: a shot that is not returned and wins the point

Further Reading & Websites

Drewett, Jim. *How to Improve at Tennis*. New York: Crabtree, 2007.

King, Donna. *Game, Set, and Match*. Boston: Kingfisher, 2007.

Sanchez Vicario, Arantxa. *The Young Tennis Player*. New York: DK Children, 1996.

Maria's Website
http://www.mariasharapova.com
Maria's official website features trivia, photos, records, and information about Maria and the United States Tennis Association.

Sports Illustrated for Kids
http://www.sikids.com
The *Sports Illustrated for Kids* website covers all sports, including tennis.

United States Tennis Association
http://www.usta.com
The USTA's website provides fans with recent news stories, statistics, schedules, and biographies of players.

Women's Tennis Association
http://www.sonyericssonwtatour.com
The WTA's website features information about players, tournaments, rules, and rankings.

Index

Australian Open, 18, 21, 26

Bollettieri, Nick, 11, 12

Eisenbud, Max (agent), 13

French Open, 21, 26

Grand Slam tournaments, 5, 18, 19, 21, 24–25. *See also* Australian Open, French Open, U.S. Open, Wimbledon

Henin, Justine, 5–8

Lansdorp, Robert, 15

Navratilova, Martina, 10–11

Seles, Monica, 11, 17

Sharapova, Maria: childhood of, 9-11; fame of, 5, 15, 23, 26–27; and junior tennis events, 14–16; professional career of, 4–8, 16–17, 18–20, 21–22, 24–26; training of, 11, 13, 14–16, 24

Sharapova, Yelena (mother), 9, 12

Sharapova, Yuri (father), 9–13, 20

U.S. Open: 2003, 19; 2006, 4–8, 25; 2007, 26

Wimbledon, 19, 21–22, 26

Photo Acknowledgments

The images in this book are used with the permission of: © Stan Honda/AFP/Getty Image, p. 4; © Don Emmert/AFP/Getty Images, pp. 6, 29; © Matthew Stockman/Getty Images, p. 7; © Harry DiOrio/Getty Images, p. 8; © Sergei Ilnitsky/epa/Corbis, p. 9; © Dean Treml/Getty Images, p. 10; © Art Seitz, pp. 12, 14, 17; © Clive Brunskill/Getty Images, p. 18; AP Photo/Dave Caulkin, p. 19; © Peter Parks/AFP/Getty Images, p. 20; © Michael Cole/Corbis, p. 22; © Toby Melville/Reuters/Corbis, p. 24; AP Photo/Andrew Brownbill, p. 27.

Front cover: © ANDREES LATIF/Corbis